LEONARDO'S SPIRITUAL STATURE

at the Turning Point of Modern Times

Rudolf Steiner

From Rudolf Steiner: *Ergebnisse der Geistesforschung*.
(Some Results of Spiritual Research).
GA 62. Lecture XI, 13th February 1913 in Berlin.

Translated by Peter Stebbing

Lecture translated from the German by Peter Stebbing
Cover design: Peter Stebbing
Cover illustration: Leonardo: "The Last Supper" (detail, restored version)

The "A" Initial graphic was designed by Rudolf Steiner

Rudolf Steiner Archive & e.Lib
Visit the website at https://www.rsarchive.org/

Printed in the United States of America

First Printing: July 2019
The e.Lib, Inc.
Rudolf Steiner Publications

ISBN-13: 978-1-948302-09-8
ISBN-10: 1-948302-09-8

We can say that he [Leonardo] bore within him the whole spirit of his age, and yet he was often misunderstood or out of sync with his time, precisely because he was already working out of the depths of the spirit, making use of powers that were only to emerge in later centuries.

Rudolf Steiner, GA 292.

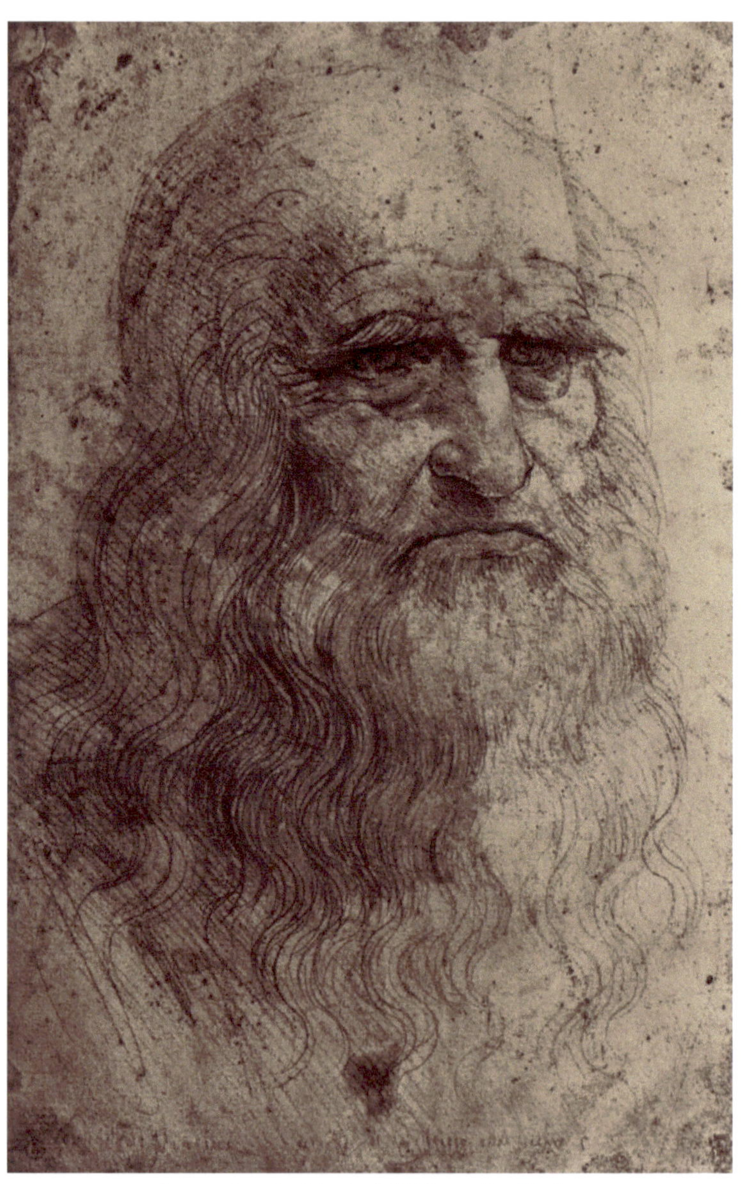

Leonardo da Vinci: Self-Portrait, Turin
Conte crayon on paper, 33,3 x 21,4 cm

LEONARDO'S SPIRITUAL STATURE

at the Turning Point of Modern Times

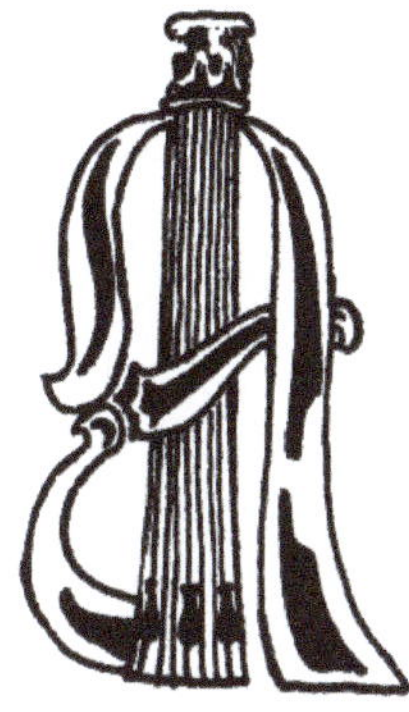

s a result of the distribution of what is perhaps the most widely known picture of all, the famous "Last Supper," Leonardo's name is continually brought to the attention of countless human souls. Who does not know it, this Last Supper of Leonardo da Vinci? And who, knowing it, has not marvelled at the tremendous idea that comes to expression in this picture! Vividly personified, we see a significant moment, a moment felt by many people as being one of the most significant in world history: The Christ figure in the middle, the twelve apostles of Christ Jesus arranged on either side. We see these twelve apostles with profoundly expressive movements and gestures. With each of the twelve figures their gestures and bearing are so individualized that we have the impression: every possible human soul characteristic comes to expression in these figures, every manner in which an individual of whatever temperament or character might respond to what the picture represents.

In his discourse on "Leonardo da Vinci's Last Supper," Goethe refers strikingly to the moment in which Christ Jesus spoke the words, "There is one among you who will betray me!"

After these words have been uttered we see what goes on in each of the twelve — so intimately associated with the speaker, who look up to Him so reverently — we see all this in the numerous reproductions of this work distributed throughout the world.

There are depictions of the Last Supper event deriving from an earlier time. Going no further back than the period from Giotto to Leonardo da Vinci, we find that, in depicting the Last Supper, Leonardo introduced what can be called the dramatic element. Indeed, a wonderfully dramatic moment presents itself in his picture. Earlier, calmer representations seem to express as it were no more than the coming together of the apostles. With dramatic power, in his "Last Supper" Leonardo graphically conjures before us for the first time an expression of the most significant soul configuration. However, having received this impression of the underlying idea of the picture in heart and mind from the world-famous reproductions, arriving in Milan, in that old Dominican church of Santa Maria delle Grazie, one sees on the wall — it cannot be described otherwise — only more or less indistinct damp patches of colour merging into each other. This is all that remains of the original painting that has become world famous through reproductions. Looking further back, one has the impression that for quite some time already it has not been possible to see much of what people witnessed after the picture had been painted by Leonardo and once spoke of in such enthusiastic, exhilarating and captivating words. What must indeed at one time have spoken to human beings from this wall as something of an artistic miracle, not only in terms of the idea that has just been haltingly enunciated, but also by virtue of Leonardo's expressive colour! In these colours the inherent nature of each soul, indeed the very heartbeat of the twelve figures must have come to expression. Yet, for a considerable time this has no longer been evident on the wall. — What has this picture not suffered in the course of time! [It should be noted that from 1978 to 1999, financed by the Olivetti Company, modern techniques of restoration have made it possible to reveal what Leonardo certifiably painted onto the wall, in so far as this remains. — And to extraordinary effect!]

Leonardo felt compelled to turn aside from the kind of technique previously employed in painting such walls. He found the painting method made use of earlier [fresco] insufficiently expressive. He wanted to conjure the subtlest emotions onto the wall. He therefore attempted to use oil-based colours, something that had not been done before in painting murals. A series of hindrances came to light. The location of the wall as well as the entire space itself was such that comparatively soon these oil colours were undermined by dampness, the moisture coming out of the wall itself. The whole room, a refectory of the Dominicans, was completely under water on one occasion as the result of flooding. Many other factors contributed to the overall problem: the billeting of troops in wartime and so forth. All these things took their toll on the picture.

There was a time in which the monks of the cloister also did not exactly conduct themselves with special piety in regard to the picture. They found the door too low that led underneath the dining hall of the cloister and one day had it made higher. In this way part of the picture was devastated. [The feet of the Saviour were eliminated.]

Then again, a heraldic shield was once placed immediately over the head of Christ: in short, the picture was treated in the most barbaric manner. And then there were charlatans — they have to be called such — who painted over the picture so that hardly anything is to be seen of the original colour it once had. Even so, standing in front of this wall painting, an indescribable magic emanates from it. In spite of all barbarity, all overpainting, all soddenness, the magic that radiates from the picture could not be entirely destroyed. Today it is only a shadow of what it once was, and yet a magical quality still proceeds from it. One can say, it is only partly the painting as such; it is also the *idea* that exerts an effect on the soul, yet this works powerfully.

We can acquaint ourselves with other works of Leonardo, by means of reproductions, or by means of the works attributed to him in various European galleries — still preserved much as he painted them. In thus getting to know Leonardo's creations, what he wrote, as well as the course of his life from 1452 to 1519, we nonetheless stand before the mural in the dining hall of the Dominicans in Milan with quite particular feelings. For, just as little remains to us of this magical creation once painted by Leonardo, little remains also for the general consciousness of humanity of the colossal stature, the power and significance of Leonardo's comprehensive personality. What can be experienced of Leonardo today barely relates otherwise to what he placed into the world than these patches of colour that merge into each other in comparison to what he once conjured onto the wall. One stands with a certain wistful melancholy before this picture in Milan; and so it is in contemplating the figure of Leonardo himself.

Goethe points out with reference to earlier biographies that one has the impression, in Leonardo a personality appeared working with fresh life forces, viewing life with joyful expectation and enthusiasm, with an enormous urge for knowledge — fresh in mind and body. Turning to the picture that counts as a self-portrait in Turin, we see a portrait of the *old* Leonardo, the countenance with expressive furrows

— expressive of pain and suffering, with the embittered mouth and features that betray much of what Leonardo must have felt in his conflicted relation to the world, in all he experienced. Strangely indeed does this personality of Leonardo stand before us at the turn of modern times.

Directing our attention once again to the picture in the Santa Maria delle Grazie we may attempt as it were with the "eye of the spirit," to use Goethe's expression, to look at this "shadow" on the wall of the refectory, comparing it with the oldest engravings, the oldest reproductions. Letting the picture re-arise for us in this way, a question can emerge for us: Did the one who once painted this picture, in making the final brush-stroke, depart from it satisfied? Did he say to himself: You have achieved what lived in your soul?

It seems to me, one arrives at this question, as a matter of course. Such a question arises of its own accord in contemplating the life of Leonardo as a whole. We see him born a natural child, the son of an average individual, Ser Pietro, in Vinci and a peasant woman who disappears from view, while the father then marries in a civil wedding and has the son fostered out. Seeing the child grow up in isolation, communing only with nature and itself, one says to oneself: a tremendous sum total of life forces must have belonged to this human being for him to remain fresh and in good health, as he did in the first place. Since he showed talent in drawing early on, he was accepted into the school of *Verrocchio* [1435-1488]. His father had brought him there, believing his talent in drawing could be exploited. The young Leonardo was now made use of in collaborating on the master's pictures. An anecdote is told from this period, that Leonardo was to paint a figure on one occasion, and that the master decided on seeing it to cease painting altogether, since he saw himself outdone by his pupil. This counts as more than an anecdote, in considering Leonardo as a complete individual.

We see him growing up in Florence, his talent in painting increasing by leaps and bounds. But we find something else. In following his painting ability, one has the feeling: Year by year he went about with the greatest artistic intentions, with continual new plans. He had commissions from people who recognized his great gifts and wanted something from him. Leonardo would first of all let the idea arise of whatever he wanted to create and then begin making studies. But how was it with these studies?

These studies proceeded from going into every conceivable detail that came into consideration — in a decidedly characteristic fashion. If he had, for example, to paint a picture in which three or four figures were to appear, he went to work in such a way that he did not merely study a single model but went about the city observing hundreds of people. He frequently followed a person for a whole day when a particular feature interested him. He would invite all kinds of people of the most varied standing to his abode, telling them all manner of things that amused or alarmed them. For, he wanted to study their features in connection with the most diverse emotional states. Once, when a rabble-rouser had been taken into custody and was to be hanged, Leonardo betook himself to the place of execution. — The drawing still exists in which he attempted to capture the facial expression and the whole gesture of the one hanged. In a lower corner of the page a head is drawn, recording the exact impression.

There are caricatures by Leonardo, incredible figures from which we can see what he actually intended. He would, for example, draw a countenance and see what would result in making the chin larger and larger. To find out what significance single parts of the human figure have, he enlarged a single member so as to discover how this fits into the whole human organism in its natural size. Grotesque figures with the most varied distortions — we find all this with Leonardo. Drawings by him exist in which he sketched a particular feature again and again — drawings he then wanted to use for corresponding works. Even if some of these derive from his students, there are still a great number from his own hand.

Letting all this work on us, we get the impression that things proceeded in such a way that he would have some commission or other for a picture; he was to depict this or that. He studied the details as described. Then something in particular began to interest him — and he then no longer studied with the aim of completing the picture, but rather to get to know specific features of an animal or of the human being. If a battle scene was to be painted, he went to the riding school to make studies — or to where the horses are left to themselves. In this way he digressed from the actual purpose for which he had intended to use the study. Studies thus pile one upon the other, till it is no longer a question of his returning to the commissioned work at all.

Among the more significant pictures in his first Florentine period — though today these have all been overpainted, their original state no longer fully recognizable — we have the "Saint Jerome" and the "Adoration of the Magi." There are studies for these as well, of the kind already indicated. One has the sense moreover that here a human being lived within the abundance of cosmic secrets. He sought to penetrate world secrets and to reproduce these secrets of Nature in an original manner by means of drawing — though never actually arriving at the kind of creating of which he could say, it had in some way been brought to realization. One has to transpose oneself into such a soul, too richly endowed to be able to fully conclude what it undertook — a soul upon which the cosmic secrets work in such a way that, in beginning somewhere, it necessarily went from secret to secret and never finished. One has to understand this Leonardo soul, too great in itself ever to be able to manifest its own greatness.

Pursuing Leonardo further in Milan, we see two tasks entrusted to him by Duke Lodovici il Moro, who takes him into his court. One task is the "Last Supper" and the other the creation of an equestrian statue of the duke's father. We see Leonardo at work on these projects for a period of fifteen to sixteen years. Yet much else transpired besides. To further characterize Leonardo and to comprehend him completely, it should be mentioned that the duke had not only appointed him as a painter. Leonardo was also an excellent musician, in fact perhaps one of the most distinguished musicians of his time. The duke was especially fond of his musical ability. But the duke also retained Leonardo because he was one of the most important war-engineers, a distinguished canal engineer and one of the most significant mechanics of his time, and because he was able to promise the duke entirely new war-machines, machines utilizing waterpower, also bridges that could easily be built and taken down again. At the same time, he worked on constructing a flying machine. In developing it, he occupied himself in observing how bird flight comes about. The studies of bird flight that have been preserved count among the most original in this field. With the writings of Leonardo, it has to be borne in mind that it is partly a matter of copies containing much that is inexact. These therefore correspond in nature to what is still to be seen today of the "Last Supper." But, shining through everywhere is the comprehensive spirit of Leonardo himself.

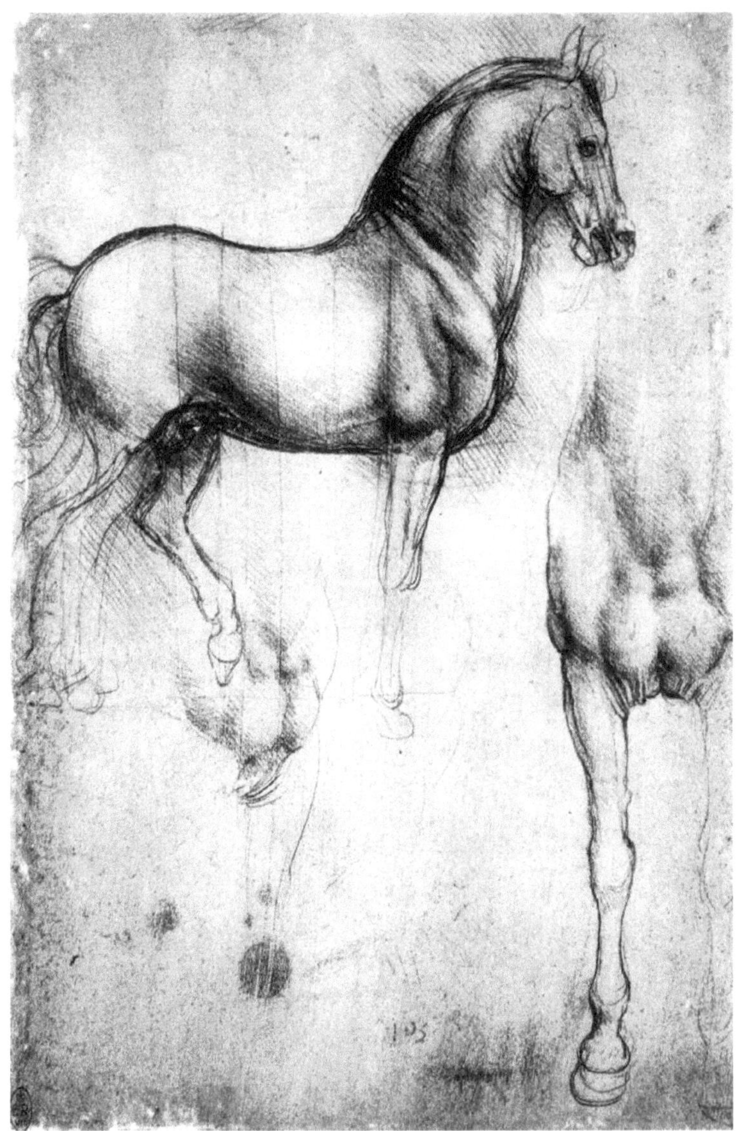

Leonardo da Vinci: Drawing of a Horse
Study for the Sforza monument
Silverpoint on prepared paper, 25 x 18,7 cm

We see Leonardo supporting the court in Milan in every conceivable way with this or that painting project or theatrical event, but also working out all manner of war plans and other plans, as also assisting in the building of the cathedral with advice and practical help. In addition, he is known to have trained numerous pupils who then worked on the various projects in Milan. Today, people hardly have any notion of all that Leonardo contributed to the city of Milan and its surroundings.

There are Leonardo's endless studies for the equestrian statue of the duke's father, Francesco Sforza. He studied every part of the animal hundreds of times in hundreds of positions, and over a period of many years he completed the model for the horse. It was destroyed when the French invaded Milan in the year 1499; soldiers shot at the model as though for target practice. Nothing of it remains — nothing is preserved of the enormous amount of work of a personality who, it may be said, sought to investigate world secrets in creating a work in which dead matter gives expression to life — just as life manifests itself with its secrets in Nature.

It is known *how* Leonardo worked on the "Last Supper." He often went there, sat on the scaffold and brooded for hours in front of the wall. Then he took the brush, made a few brushstrokes and went away again. When he wanted to paint on the Christ figure, his hand trembled. And, considering all that is known, it has to be said: both outwardly and inwardly Leonardo was not pleased as a result of painting this world-famous picture. There were people at the time in Milan who did not much like the slow pace with which the picture was painted. There was for instance the prior of the cloister who could not see why a painter should not be able to paint such a picture onto the wall quite quickly. He complained to the duke. For the duke, the whole matter also went on rather too long, and he took the artist to task. Leonardo replied that Christ Jesus and Judas were to be represented in the picture: two of the greatest imaginable contrasts. These could not be painted in just one year, there being no model for either in the whole world, not for Judas, nor for Christ Jesus. He also did not know, he said, having painted on the picture for many years already, whether he would be able to finish it at all. And then he added: In the end, if no model were found for Judas, he could always take the prior! Thus, it was extraordinarily difficult to bring the picture to a conclusion. But Leonardo was also not pleased in the end with the outcome. For, with this picture the full discrepancy became apparent between what lived in his soul and what he was able to bring onto the wall.

Here I am obliged to put forward a kind of spiritual-scientific hypothesis to which anyone can come on familiarizing themselves gradually with all that can be known about the picture. This hypothesis resulted for me in attempting to answer the question previously raised. In following the life of Leonardo, one says to oneself: Such an enormous amount lived in this man that he was unable to reveal outwardly to humanity — for which the external means were wholly inadequate. Should he in fact have been able, without further ado, to paint to his satisfaction the greatest conceivable work he undoubtedly intended with the "Last Supper?" One comes to such a question as a matter of course, seeing how he strove again and again by means of studies, to investigate one secret after another — attempting to bring something to realization that did not finally come about. And the answer then results almost of itself. For, if Leonardo had wanted on the one hand to make an equestrian statue, a miraculous work of sculpture, bringing it no further than the model that was lost, never reaching the point of casting it after sixteen years' work — having to forsake it completely without achieving anything — how must he have taken leave of the "Last Supper?" One has the sense that he went away from it dissatisfied! And today we have only a ruin of the picture before us; only damp patches of colour merging into each other, while for a long time hardly anything is left of what Leonardo once painted onto the wall. Thus, it is perhaps permissible to assert that what he painted onto the wall did not remotely represent what lived in his soul.

To arrive at such an impression, however, one has to bear in mind various things in regard to the picture. There are further reasons. Among the various writings of Leonardo that have survived there is a wonderful *Treatise on Painting*. [See Dover Publications edition, 2005.] Here the essential nature of painting as an art is set forth — how perspective and colour composition are to be approached. It is shown that one needs to proceed from a certain viewpoint. Despite the fact that we have it only in a truncated form, this book by Leonardo on painting is a wonderful work, like nothing else that has been written on painting otherwise. The principles of the art of painting are presented as only the greatest genius could have presented them. It is marvellous, for instance, to read how Leonardo describes in what manner horses are to be depicted in a battle scene, how altogether brutal, but also grandiose impressions are to come to light in rendering a battle scene. In short, this work shows Leonardo in his greatness and, it may be said, also in a certain powerlessness, which we shall refer to later. But above all, it betrays how he was careful everywhere in his own painting to study how reality presents itself to the human eye; how light-and-dark and colouration are to be utilized — all this is set forth in genial fashion in this work of Leonardo on painting. And it confirms the yearning for *conscience* in Leonard's soul, the desire, never even in the slightest detail, to go against what, as we shall see, he valued so highly: the search for truth. The extent to which this lived in his soul becomes apparent everywhere in the *Treatise on Painting;* in that one should never violate the truth of the impression with respect to the inner secrets of Nature.

Letting his "Last Supper" work on us, there are two things we cannot reconcile immediately with Leonardo's requirements with regard to painting. One concerns the figure of Judas. In the reproductions and to an extant in the shadowy picture in Milan, one has the impression, Judas is completely covered in shadow and is quite dark. Looking at how the light falls from various sides, with the eleven other disciples we see the relationships of light everywhere represented in the most wonderful way in conformity with the truth. Nothing properly explains the darkness on the countenance of Judas! On the basis of the external relationships of light we do not have a satisfying answer as to the "why" of this darkness. And in coming to the Christ-Jesus figure, if one does not proceed on the basis of spiritual science, only something like a premonition can actually result for external perception. For just as little as the blackness, the darkness, is outwardly justified, as little does the sun-like quality of the Christ figure, its emergence from the other figures, seem justified in the sense indicated. All the other countenances can be understood on the basis of the existing lighting, but not the Judas and not the Christ-Jesus countenance. Proceeding in accordance with spiritual science, however, the thought arises as though of itself: here the painter strove to make evident, in the contrast of "Jesus" and "Judas," how light and darkness are to be accounted for *inwardly*. He wanted to make clear that this Christ countenance stands before us, such that we find it unaccounted for in regard to the external light, but that we are able to believe: the soul behind this countenance grants it luminosity of itself, so that it becomes permissible for it to shine in contradiction to the prevailing light conditions. And in the same way, one has the impression with regard to Judas, this figure conjures a shadow onto itself justified by nothing in the surroundings.

As already stated, this is a spiritual-scientific hypothesis, but one that has emerged for me over many years, a hypothesis of which one can believe that it will confirm itself still further, the more one goes into the whole matter. On the basis of this hypothesis, one understands that in striving everywhere in his work for the truth of Nature, Leonardo worked with a brush that trembled in his hand in attempting to present what could have its justification only in the Christ figure. It becomes comprehensible that Leonardo would unquestionably have been bitterly disappointed, since it was impossible, with the art of representation as it was at the time, to bring this to expression in all truthfulness. Thus, he could not do what he intended, and finally despaired of the possibility of carrying it out, having to bequeath a picture which did not ultimately satisfy him.

Thus, in conformity with the entire spiritual stature of Leonardo, we arrive at an answer to the above question. Leonardo must have gone from this picture with the bitter feeling that with his most significant work, he had set himself a task the execution of which could not bring him satisfaction, given the means available. Though in later centuries no human eye was in fact to see what Leonardo had actually conjured onto the wall in Milan, even in his own time the picture did not correspond with what had lived in his soul. Hence, considering him in relation to his most important creation, we are inclined to ask: what really is the underlying secret of this figure of Leonardo?

In contemplating the personality of Raphael fourteen days ago, the attempt was made to show that, based on a spiritual-scientific view, such a unique individual can be understood quite differently than otherwise. We can make clear to ourselves that the human soul returns again and again in the course of many earth-lives. Born into a particular age, a soul does not live this one life only, but, with its whole disposition, brings qualities over from earlier earth-lives. With what it carries over into the present from earlier lives, the soul interacts with what the spiritual environment has to offer. Viewing the human soul in this way, we recognize that it enters into existence with an inner spiritual estate deriving from repeated earth-lives. The whole of evolution appears meaningful and imbued with wisdom in presupposing that things arise in particular epochs, not by chance, but according to law-imbued principles — just as the blossom of the plant follows after the green leaves. Great individualities become explicable only if we assume wise guidance in the historical development of humanity and see the human soul returning again and again from spiritual regions. But what can be studied in the context of a single human life unveils itself quite especially in considering human souls that rise above mediocrity. Contemplating Leonardo in the way we attempted in tentatively summarizing his life, we are inevitably led again and again to the background from which he emerges. This is the age into which he is placed, from the year 1452 to the year 1519.

What sort of age is this? It is the age that precedes the flowering of the natural-scientific worldview — before the arrival of the worldview of Copernicus and before Giordano Bruno, Kepler and Galileo. How is this age to be viewed from a spiritual-scientific standpoint?

We have often drawn attention to the fact that the further we go back in evolution, the more the whole manner in which human beings relate to the world changes. In primeval times we find everywhere a kind of clairvoyance. In certain states between sleeping and waking, human beings looked into the spiritual world. This original clairvoyance was lost as time went on, but even in the fifteenth century a remnant of this clairvoyance remained from older times. It was not then a matter of the actual clairvoyance itself, which had long since been lost. What remained was a feeling of the soul's connection with the spiritual background of the world. What souls had once seen, they continued to feel. Though this feeling had become weak, they nonetheless felt united in the centre of their being with the spiritual element with which the world was permeated and interwoven — much as physical processes in the human body are connected with physical occurrences in the world.

It belongs to the inherent laws of evolution that the old connection of the human soul with the spiritual world had to be lost for a while. Never would modern natural science have been able to blossom, had the old clairvoyance remained. This older way of seeing had to be lost, in order for human beings to orient themselves to what is presented to the senses, to reason bound up with the brain — to what can be ascertained scientifically. Only by virtue of the loss of the old spiritual perception was the natural scientific world conception possible that has evolved from the time of Leonardo up to our own day. In this way human beings turned "objectively," as it is said, to the external sense world and to what human reason is able to comprehend by means of sense perception.

Today we stand once more at a new turning point, at the turning point of a time in which it is again possible, by means of modern natural science, for human beings to come to a spiritual view of things. For, the development of natural science has a dual significance. On the one hand, it is to bequeath to humanity a certain wealth of natural-scientific knowledge. In the course of the centuries since the appearance of Copernicus, Kepler and so on, natural science has gone from triumph to triumph, influencing in a remarkable way all practical and theoretical life. That is one field that has been conquered by natural science in the centuries since Leonardo's time. The other is something that could not come about all at once and has become possible only in our time. Not only do we owe to natural science what has been learned as a result of the Copernican worldview, by means of the observations and investigations of Kepler and Galileo, as also what has been discovered by means of modern spectral analysis and so forth. We are indebted to it also for a certain education of the human soul.

Human beings directed their attention first of all to the sense world. Natural science evolved in this way. But new ideas, new concepts were formed by means of natural science. And where natural science achieved the most significant advances, it did not do so by means of sense perception, but by virtue of something quite different. This has already been pointed out. In a particular field prior to Copernicus, reliance was placed on sense perception. What was the result? It was believed, the earth stood still in cosmic space and the sun and other planets circled around it. Then came Copernicus, who had the courage not to rely on sense observation. He had the courage to say that no empirical discoveries are made in relying on sense perception alone, but that empirical discoveries are arrived at in combining in a strict manner in one's thinking all that has previously been observed. People then followed in his footsteps; and it misconstrues the actual facts altogether to believe that natural science attained its present height in that humanity placed reliance only on the senses.

But what humanity acquired by means of natural science also imprinted itself on souls. The ideas of natural science live in our souls, exerting an educational effect. Quite apart from their content, the natural sciences have been an educational medium. And today, in that natural scientific ideas are actually not only thought but also lived, human beings have become ready of themselves to feel drawn to spiritual science. Humanity had first to become mature for this. The centuries since the time of Leonardo had to pass for this to come about.

Now let us consider Leonardo. He enters an age having, in an earlier existence, belonged among those initiates who had elevated themselves in the ancient manner to apprehending the secrets of the universe. Born into the fifteenth century, he could not bring this to realization. Though someone may have entered intensely into the cosmic secrets in earlier incarnations, as made possible in those earlier earth-lives, how this is to be brought to consciousness in a new existence depends upon the external corporeality. A physical body of the fifteenth century could not bring to expression what Leonardo had assimilated in an earlier existence of inner thoughts, inner feelings and creative power. What he had brought with him from earlier times took effect only in the form of a certain strength. In the age preceding the flowering of the natural sciences, he felt constrained by a body that placed limits upon him. The times were approaching — the dawn of which had already arrived — when people wanted only to look into the world of sense and to think only by means of reason bound to the instrument of the brain. Leonardo felt drawn everywhere to the spirit, having brought this with him as an impulse from earlier lives. In a grandiose manner, he was impelled to the spirit.

Let us now look at him as an artist in the first place. Art had become quite different in the age in which Leonardo lived from what it was for instance in Greek times. We may attempt to transpose ourselves, for example, into how a Greek artist created a sculptural figure. What kind of feeling do we have in looking even at the statue of Marcus Aurelius [175 A.D.] in Rome? Never would those who created something like this have proceeded in the manner of Michelangelo or Leonardo, making detailed studies from an external model. The wonderful horse of the Marcus Aurelius statue was quite certainly not studied in the way Leonardo went about studying his horse for the equestrian statue of Francesco Sforza. How alive are these ancient statues even so! Why is this? It derives from the fact that in Greek times human beings felt themselves the immediate creators of their own bodies, feeling themselves at one with the soul forces of the cosmos. In the times when Greek art arose, one sensed, for example with an arm, all the forces that formed it. One felt one's way into the inner, self-sufficient nature of one's own human form. Things were not viewed from outside, but created from within, while being aware of the actual formative forces. This can even be established quite externally. Taking a look at Greek female figures, we find they are all directly felt. Hence, they are shown at an age when growth is ascendant. Here we sense that the artist created as Nature does, in standing within the spirit of Nature, feeling himself inwardly connected with the spirit of Nature.

This feeling of union with the spirit that lives and weaves through things had been lost in the age of Leonardo. It had to be so, since it would not have been possible otherwise for modern times to arise. This is said not as a critique of the times, but to indicate the underlying facts.

Let us look at how Leonardo went to work in studying say, the movements of the hand, the parts of an animal, or the human physiognomy. He proceeds in having a notion, an inner experience that does not, however, rise to consciousness. This is something that is brought to bear in a living manner in creating these figures, but Leonardo cannot apprehend it from within. He feels as though detached from it, from apprehending it inwardly. And now nothing is sufficient for him. The new natural scientific worldview does not yet exist. He stands there in expectation of this natural scientific worldview, without as yet having it for himself. With his writings, things jump out on every page that are only discovered over the next three hundred years, and in some cases have still not been found even today. Leonardo had the most wonderful ideas that frequently had no effect at all in his own time. We find these ideas both in his written works and in his artistic creations.

Thus, with him we sense the helplessness with which a soul had to appear in an age in which the old way of conceiving things came to an end, and for whom the new world conception had not yet arisen. But this new world conception brought with it that the whole outlook of human beings became splintered, in focussing on details. We see a specialization of the different branches of work. With Leonardo everything still appears unified. He is at the same time fully a painter, fully a musician, fully a philosopher, fully a technician. He united these within himself, having come over from ancient times with great capacities. In the new age he is able everywhere to touch on things, but not to enter into them. And so, in human terms, Leonardo appears as a tragic figure. But, seen from a higher point of view, he is enormously significant, appearing at the turning point of a new age.

One sees this in looking at Leonardo's further achievements. The most significant things were brought by him only up to a certain point; then his students worked on them. And even in the case of such works as the "Saint John" or the "Mona Lisa" in the Louvre in Paris, we see that, in consequence of the technical means by which they were produced, they soon lost their lustre. We also see how Leonardo could never be satisfied. Without having the pictures to hand, it is not possible to speak about Leonardo's paintings in detail. Immersing oneself in them, it becomes evident that as an artist Leonardo continually came up against boundaries that he could not surmount. We see how what lived in his soul could not reach the point where from the state of soul experience, it lit up in his consciousness. In lighting up at a certain moment from the level of soul experience in this way, one could shout for joy, but sinks back in pain, since it does not reach clear consciousness. Even for Leonardo himself, this did not come about.

We actually follow Leonardo with rather bitter feelings in seeing how he is sent for by Francis I [king of France from 1515-1547] and, for the last three years of his life, in the residence Francis I had assigned him, spends these years in spiritual contemplation, immersed in the secrets of existence. We encounter him there as a lonely individual who cannot actually any longer have had anything much in common with the world that surrounded him; who had to sense a tremendous contrast between what he felt to be the primal foundation of existence, capable of taking on form by means of art, and what he had been able to bequeath to the world after all only in fragmentary form.

Recognizing this with regard to Leonardo one says to oneself: This is an individual in whom much takes place; an infinite amount goes on in his soul. The impression made on the observer is shattering — considering what is given over to humanity, what is revealed to humanity externally at Leonardo's death and how slight this is, compared to what lived within him! How does it stand with the economy of existence, if we subscribe to the view that human life exhausts itself in what comes into existence externally? How meaningless and pointless does the soul-life of such an individual as Leonardo appear when we see all that went on within him in relation to what he was able to bequeath to the world? What contradiction would result in asserting: this individual may be viewed only in accordance with how he manifested himself in outer life! *No,* we cannot view such a soul in this way! We must adopt a different standpoint and say: Whatever Leonardo may have given to the world, what he experienced, what he went through inwardly — all that belongs to another world, a supersensible world as compared to our world. And such human beings are above all evidence that, with his soul, the human being stands within supersensible existence. We can say, such souls achieve something of significance with regard to supersensible existence, while what they leave to the world is only a "by-product" of what they undergo otherwise.

We only arrive at a true impression in adding to the stream of external human events, another, a supersensible stream, saying: Something takes place parallel to the sense-perceptible stream, and souls are in fact embedded in the supersensible realm. They live within this realm so as to be the connecting link between the sensible and the supersensible. The existence of such souls as Leonardo's appears meaningful only when we are able to accept the existence of a supersensible realm in which they are embedded. Thus, we apprehend little of Leonardo in looking only at what results from his creative activity. We arrive at the view that this soul still has something to sort out in supersensible existence. We can then say to ourselves: We understand! — In order to be able to reveal various things to humanity over the course of many earth-lives, this soul had to undergo, in that "Leonardo existence," the circumstance that only the least of what lived within it could come to outer expression. Thus, individuals such as Leonardo are themselves real life-enigmas, embodying cosmic riddles.

What I wanted to put forward today should not be presented in sharply defined concepts. The intention has been rather to provide indications as to how such souls may be approached. Truly, the task of spiritual science is not to provide theories! In all it is capable of, spiritual science should take hold of the entire feeling life of human beings and become an elixir of life — enabling us to gain a new relationship to the world and to life. Spirits such as Leonardo are quite especially suited to make this possibility clear to us. Contemplating spirits like Leonardo, we can say: They enter existence mysteriously, having something of greater importance to express than their age is capable of supporting. Bringing over treasures from earlier times, individuals such as Leonardo enter life in unprepossessing circumstances. Born of an average father and a mother who soon disappears from one's field of vision altogether, having given birth to a natural child, Leonardo was subsequently brought up by average people. Thus, we see him left to himself, yet bringing to expression what he had carried over from earlier lives. In looking at the unfavourable circumstances of his birth, we recognize that they did not prevent the greatest imaginable content of soul from manifesting itself.

We see Leonardo in good health, so complete in himself that it becomes understandable when Goethe states: "Of regular features, well-formed, he stood before humanity as an exemplary human being. And just as the eye's clarity and power of comprehension belong in reality to reason, to the power of judgement, so clarity and comprehension were integral to this artist." In making use of these words with reference to Leonardo, and they are applicable to him, we can apply them to the youthful Leonardo. We encounter him, fresh in mind and body, full of creative enthusiasm, of a kind of cosmic yearning — a complete human being, an exemplary human being. He is as though born a conqueror, yet likewise born with humour, which he showed on the most diverse occasions. Turning once again to the drawing that rightly counts as a self-portrait, to the old man in whose countenance so much is engraved of painful experience, leaving deep furrows, we see the features around the mouth indicating disharmony. He is ultimately a lonely man, far from his fatherland, living in asylum, at the behest of the king of France — still struggling with questions of cosmic existence — but alone, forsaken, not understood, though appreciated by loyal friends who accompanied him.

Hence the greatness of this spirit presents itself to us as having undergone much suffering, initially entering into life fully, and then departing from it embittered. We look into this countenance and sense the genius of humanity itself looking out from this human countenance. We begin to understand the age, the evening glow in which Leonardo lived, as also the age in which Copernicus, Kepler, Giordano Bruno and Galileo lived — in which a new dawn breaks. We take note of all the limitations and restrictions Leonardo's great soul had to endure. In comprehending the age, we understand this great artist who could ultimately only work with the means available. Looking into Leonardo's countenance with our full powers of understanding, while immersing ourselves in spiritual scientific viewpoints, it is as though the whole character of the age looks out from this countenance. These embittered facial features express indeed in the first place something of the downward inclination of the human spirit. We need to acquaint ourselves with this aspect of Leonardo in order to become aware of the magnitude of the power that had to be there for a Copernicus, a Kepler, a Galileo, a Giordano Bruno to arise.

Actually, we only acquire the proper reverence with respect to the development of the human spirit in feeling the tragedy of Giordano Bruno's being burned at the stake; and also, in learning to deepen this in viewing the powerlessness felt by Leonardo in the preceding, declining age. Leonardo's greatness only becomes clear to us in having a sense for what he was not able to accomplish. And this is connected with something with which we wish to summarize and conclude today's considerations. It is connected with the fact that the human soul can be satisfied after all, even animated, in viewing imperfections — if not so much in viewing small imperfections, nonetheless in viewing the large imperfections where creative activity, on account of its greatness, "dies" in the execution. For, in such "dying" forces we surmise and finally recognize forces that prepare the future. And in the evening glow there arises for us the premonition and the hope of the coming dawn.

In regard to the evolution of humanity we must at all times feel able to say to ourselves, all development takes its course in such a way that wherever what has been created becomes a ruin, we know that out of the ruins new life will always blossom forth.

–Translated by Peter Stebbing
June 2018

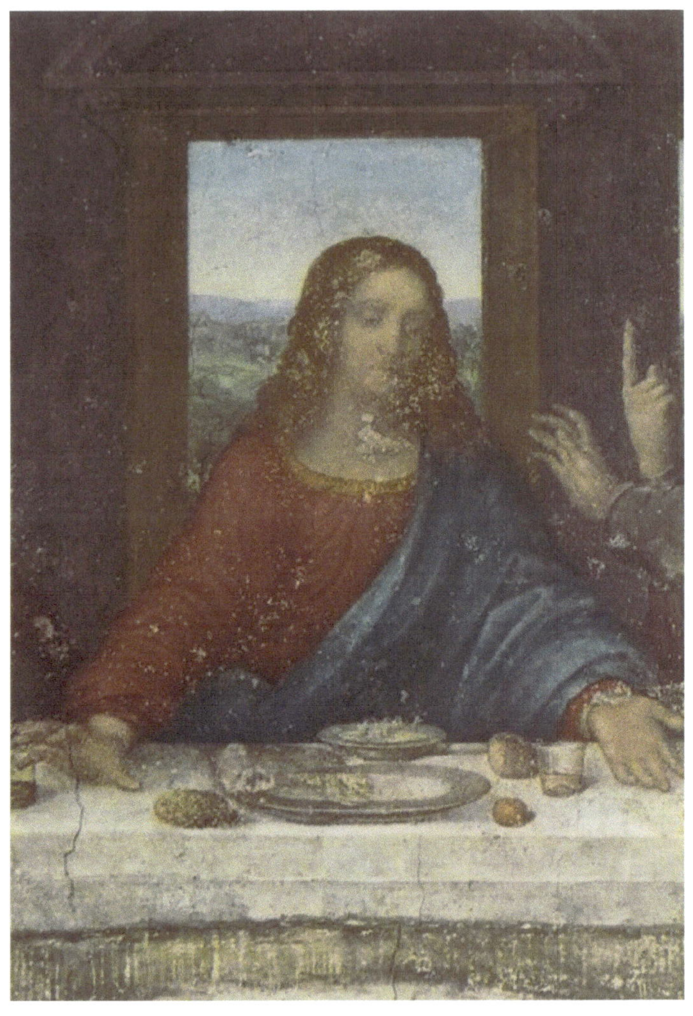

Leonardo's Last Supper, detail, the central figure of Christ
In the earlier overpainted state, seen by Rudolf Steiner

The extent to which the picture was distorted by overpainting becomes evident in comparing this with the restored version reproduced on the front cover.

On-line Activities

- On-line Search of Bn/GA# 62 texts
- On-line Compare of Bn/GA# 62 texts
- Rudolf Steiner Archive & e.Lib. *The History of Art* part 1, Bn/GA# 292 translated by Christian van Arnim.
- Rudolf Steiner Archive & e.Lib. *The History of Art* part 2, Bn/GA# 292 translated by Hanna von Maltitz.
- Fine Art Presentations – e.Gallery. *Leonardo* (Leonardo da Vinci)
- Fine Art Presentations – e.Gallery. *Raphael* (Raffaello Sanzio)

About the translator

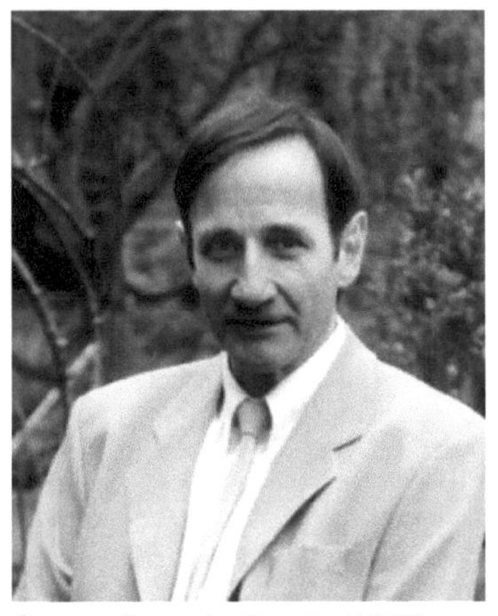

Born in Copenhagen, Denmark in 1941, Peter Stebbing attended Waldorf Schools in England. Having studied at art schools in Brighton and London, he emigrated to the United States in 1966, continuing his studies at Cornell University and earning the M.F.A. degree in painting in 1968.

While teaching design and colour courses over a period of six years in the City University of New York, he began a practical exploration of the scientific colour phenomena set forth by Goethe in his colour theory. This led eventually to a turning point – to the crucial question of finding a correspondingly lawful approach to colour in painting.

The new and wholly different training in colour experience begun in 1976 with the painter Gerard Wagner on the basis of Rudolf Steiner's motif sketches, resolved fundamental artistic questions with a coherent and systematic approach. Fully in accord with Goethe's discoveries and method, this approach may be termed "Goetheanistic."

Peter Stebbing subsequently established a painting school

at the Threefold Educational Foundation in Spring Valley, N.Y., teaching there from 1983 until 1990. Since 1992 he has been director of the Arteum Painting School (http://www.arteum-malschule.de/) in Dornach, Switzerland. He is also the translator and editor of various anthroposophical art publications.

Other books translated and edited by Peter Stebbing

- Margarita Woloschin, *The Green Snake. An Autobiography*. Floris Books, 2010. 431 pages paperback.
- Elisabeth Wagner-Koch and Gerard Wagner, *The Individuality of Colour. Contributions to a Methodical Schooling in Colour Experience*. 2nd edition. 128 pages. Hardcover. Rudolf Steiner Press, 2009.
- *The Goetheanum Cupola Motifs of Rudolf Steiner. Paintings by Gerard Wagner*. 236 pages. Hardcover. SteinerBooks, 2011.
- *Conversations about Painting with Rudolf Steiner. Recollections of Five Pioneers of the New Art Impulse*. 195 pages, 77 illustrations, hardcover. Steinerbooks, 2008.
- *Three Grimms' Fairy Tales. Paintings by Gerard Wagner*. 70 pages with 31 colour plates, hardcover. SteinerBooks, 2012.
- Rudolf Steiner, *The World of Fairy Tales*. 23 black-and-white shaded drawings by Gerard Wagner. 124 pages, paperback. SteinerBooks 2013.
- *The Art of Colour and the Human Form: Seven Motif Sketches of Rudolf Steiner: Studies by Gerard Wagner*. 218 pages, hardcover. Verlag des Ita Wegman Instituts, 2017. Also available from SteinerBooks, Great Barrington, USA.

www.ingramcontent.com/pod-product-compliance
Lightning Source LLC
LaVergne TN
LVHW052301100826
845147LV00001B/112

9781948302098